DEAR
GRETA GARBO

DEAR
GRETA GARBO

A novel by Toby Talbot

G. P. Putnam's Sons/New York

Library of Congress Cataloging in Publication Data
Talbot, Toby. Dear Greta Garbo.
SUMMARY: Thirteen-year-old Miranda and her recently
widowed grandmother find that they share similar
identity and growth problems.
[1. Grandmothers—Fiction.   2. Family life—
Fiction]   I. Title.
PZ7.T148De   [Fic]   77-14383
ISBN 0-399-20613-2

For Sarah, with love

DEAR
GRETA GARBO

ONE

Miranda, lying on the itchy September grass, yanked a little clump of lemon thyme from her mother's herb garden and rubbed it between her fingers. *The dryer it gets, the stronger it smells,* she thought. A flock of Canadian geese drove overhead in V lineup, honking in their annual fall passage over Long Island.

Miranda craned her head to get a good view of them. *Lucky ducks,* she said to herself. *Not only can they fly, but they're on their way south. Not like me. The only place I'll be heading for is the Long Island Expressway, straight back to New York and—ugh!—school.*

How she dreaded summer's end, leaving behind

the free and easy days, having to crank up a new momentum, one of alarm clocks, schedules, demands. These obnoxious thoughts drove her into the house where she took a jar of beach plum jelly from its pantry jail and came back outside. She collapsed into the hammock and began eating the jam with her finger, taking secret satisfaction out of the mess she was making on her white shirt. She could hear her mother complaining, "Fruit spots stain."

Lately her mother had been awfully picky. In any ordinary day she could reel off a laundry list of Miranda's faults, forcing Miranda to defend herself with a dozen lame excuses.

"Miranda, can't you use your knife and fork for eating?" Defense: "But if it's O. K. to eat chicken and lamb chops with your fingers, why not pork chops?" "Pork chops are too greasy." "Why do you serve your family greasy food?" Miranda always tried to get the last word.

Or: "Miranda, must you waste your whole evening on the telephone?" "I'm not wasting it, I'm talking to my friends." "Isn't the daytime long enough for that?" "We're doing our homework together." "What kind of way is that to do homework? When *I* went to school . . ."

Or: "Miranda, for heaven's sake, why must you wear your blue jeans so long they drag on the ground and get tattered at the cuffs?" To that, Miranda only gave a disgusted glance at her mother's pants flapping a full inch above her shoes, looking like some sorry hand-me-downs from an older sister. How could you *explain* to someone the perfect length for pants? There were some things people either picked up on or didn't.

Anyhow, for some reason Miranda hesitated these days to talk about certain things with her mother, like pimples, or how fat her thighs were, or how flat her chest was, which she knew her mother would find silly. Her mother was always so busy, so organized, fitting thousands of things into her life—her job, gardening, watercolors, baking bread and the best sacher tortes this side of Vienna, devoting herself to ecology—serious concerns.

Sometimes it made Miranda feel as if she and her mother were drawing apart. Yet, the truth was that Miranda herself felt secret tugs to break away and found herself balking at certain routines, certain expectations that her mother had of her. Little-girl expectations. As if she didn't realize that at thirteen Miranda was growing up. Miranda sighed. Oh, how she wished it would happen already. Growing up was like waiting for that first snow. It seemed as if it would never happen.

Miranda's sister Sonya was lucky. Last week

she'd gone off to college in Colorado and was now free. For years, during every battle between them, Miranda had looked forward to this moment when her older sister would scat, not so much because of their squabbles, which were no more frequent or infrequent than those of other sisters, but because Miranda could have Sonya's room. Miranda couldn't wait to get out of her own little room, which visitors called cozy and cute (How she loathed that word!), but which she had lately begun to think of as a dingy cell, a mole's tunnel outgrown.

For years Miranda had looked forward to being the only child at home, enjoying her parents' undivided attention, sharing more of their treats. Now the idea of remaining as their single target, the sole victim for them to zero in on, sent her into a cold sweat and made her tongue go furry (or, was it all that plum jam?).

Her thoughts were abruptly interrupted.

"Mir-aaan-da."

Her mother's voice yodeled out from the house, as if she were calling in the pigs. Miranda didn't answer. She shoved the empty jar under her towel.

Again: "Miranda."

What chore did her mother have up her sleeve now? *Please throw out the garbage. Would you mind peeling and slicing these apples for a Brown*

Betty? Could you dump these coffee grinds into the compost heap? Would you bicycle over to the store for a container of milk? Or, nastiest of all: *Would you grate these onions, dear?* Miranda stared, glazed-eyed, at the sky lacing through the maple branches overhead.

"Miranda!"

"Yes, Mom." Persistence rewarded.

"Where are you?"

"Out here?"

"Where's here?"

"In the hammock."

In a moment her mother appeared alongside the hammock. Before she could say anything, Miranda licked her sticky lips and said, "Say, Mom, the plum jam this year is terrific. The best you've ever made."

To her surprise her mother didn't comment on the splotch on Miranda's shirt or chide her for eating jam before dinner. Instead, she smiled. "How'd you like to go for a bicycle ride with me? On the way back we can gather potatoes."

Miranda felt like a blob under her blue jeans and didn't want to budge, but her mother looked so sunny and hopeful, Miranda didn't have the heart to turn her down. After all, she couldn't ask Sonya. Sonya was in Colorado. And she couldn't ask Miranda's father. He was in the city.

They mounted their bicycles and headed for the sea. Her mother pedaled vigorously for someone her age, rising high in her seat, her hair flying. To look at her, you'd never guess she was a school librarian, like her own mother used to be. Miranda wondered if her mother expected *her* to be a librarian. Every year at Christmastime she gave Miranda a subscription to *National Geographic*. Miranda knew more about Afghanistan and Peru than she knew about Brooklyn. She sighed and pedaled faster.

They rode along Benson Lane, the oldest road in Greenville, Long Island, founded in 1638. Squinting into the sun, Miranda looked out at the cabbage fields on one side, with the leathery green rosettes embroidering the brown earth, and the cornfields on the other, rows and rows of erect stalks bulging with tasseled ears of ripe corn. On and on they rode, past familiar wooden shingled houses, weathered barns, the seventeenth-century cemetery that lolled on a slope, sheltering little stone graves with ancient rubbings. Old names: Halsey, Burnett, Jennings, Hildreth, Sayre, the names of those early settlers of Long Island and their descendents. Miranda knew some of the inscriptions by heart: "Phoebe Howell who departed this life November 3rd A. D., 1801, in the 87th year of her age."

As she and her mother pedaled along, they did not talk, but her mother pointed at the sun, fat, yellow, and sprawling like a sunflower, and smiled. Miranda smiled back.

She was beginning to feel human again as the jam worked its way down all those winding canals she could picture from a diagram of the digestive tract that had flapped like a banner last term over the Biology I blackboard.

At the end of the road rose the dunes, and beyond the dunes lay the sea. Miranda and her mother strolled on the pink sand in the company of chipper sandpipers rushing back and forth with little mincing steps in their eternal comings and goings, ignoring the noisy congregation of great white gulls who stalked the beach like voracious pirates. The sea swelled in its own infinite comings and goings, and Miranda allowed the water to lap her ankles.

On the way back, she and her mother stopped at the potato field to fill the bags that her mother was carrying in her basket. The little nubby potatoes left behind by the harvester were the best. You ate them cooked in their jackets with thick salt and lumps of butter, or with garlic mayonnaise. Miranda's father loved them.

Miranda went off in one direction, her mother in another. Her bare feet plowed through the warm dry soil that had baked up the day's heat. Here and there the top of a potato peeked out of a furrow. Miranda stooped, unearthed it, tossed it into her bag. One potato led to another. Her fingers rummaged among the clods of earth, her toes burrowed into the earth. She moved back and forth across the field dappled with shadows and the falling sun. The land of Long Island was level as a tray. It looked as if it went on forever, flat as people once believed the earth to be. Far off at the other end of the field Miranda saw her mother, a silhouette in the shifting mauve light. Miranda felt a deep sense of contentment on this free open land, her mother nearby. Stoop, gather, collect. Her bag grew heavier and heavier.

As they pumped slowly home, weighed down by their loads, Miranda was happy. She was even prepared to view her return to New York, to her new room, to her city friends as something to look forward to. Maybe even school would hold some pleasant surprises. September wasn't only dry grass: it was a time of changes.

Her own room! Mentally she began transforming her sister's vacated quarters. Miranda would have twin beds so that she could invite friends for comfortable sleep-overs, a shag rug in the center to stretch out on and listen to records, a red bean chair in front of the window, a bulletin board. She would have a new open space in which to be herself.

As she and her mother steered their bicycles into the shed, the promising smell of onion soup drifted out from the kitchen. Miranda heard herself offering sweetly, "Can I help with dinner, Mom? Peel onions or something . . . ," knowing full well that the onions were already sliced and melting in their hot broth. To herself she added, *Miranda, you are a hypocrite!* And, to make amends, she quickly added aloud, "or do anything else?"

Before her mother could answer, the telephone screeched from inside. Miranda ran in to catch it before it stopped ringing. It might be her friend Emma. They were planning a farewell beach picnic for Sunday.

She picked up. "Is Mommy home?" her father asked. His voice sounded peculiar. He didn't even say hello. Imagine, her own father, acting the stranger with his daughter. Treating her like a nonperson. Familiar feelings of resentment creaked in Miranda, spoiling her mood.

"It's for you," she said cooly to her mother.

"Who is it?"

"Dad."

As her mother listened at the phone, her eyes veiled, her shoulders dropped, she seemed to shrink in size. Miranda listened to her mother's replies into the receiver and tried to decipher the one-sided conversation at this end of the wire. The clues were vague and ominous.

"We were out."

. . .

"When?"

. . .

"Where?"

. . .

"How bad is it?"

. . .

"Shall we come?"

Miranda knew it was bad news. Illness, a mugging, an automobile accident, irreversible disaster. Her mother hung up the phone, but held onto the receiver as though clinging to the connection with her husband. Her body remained in a frozen pose like a rabbit stunned in the headlights of a car.

Miranda hurried over and held her mother's shoulder. "Mommy, what is it?"

"Grandpa is very sick. Pneumonia. Daddy tried to call us earlier. We must go home."

TWO

A half hour later the tires of their car were racing over the Long Island Expressway. Never had a departure been so fast. In minutes, it seemed, Miranda's mother slammed the windows shut, turned off the flame on the soup, leaving the pot on top of the stove, locked all the doors and revved up the car motor. This time, she didn't collect armfuls of flowers, bunches of herbs and vegetables from the garden, or leftovers from the refrigerator, all the stuff they ordinarily toted back from country to city. Nor did she linger by the pond for a last look. It was a miracle that they remembered the birdcage from the back porch, for the poor parakeets would have starved or frozen to death. It was Miranda who remembered.

Once on the road, she thought of all the things she'd left undone. She'd forgotten her sneakers and her bathing suit, which she'd be needing for gym; she'd left behind a mystery she was halfway through; and she hadn't phoned Emma to cancel their beach picnic. She also found herself wondering what the onion soup would smell like when and if they returned. Her mother hardly spoke. She was buried in her own thoughts. *Why is it,* thought Miranda, *that fear pulls people apart?*

Under the wheels of the car the road flew by. Miranda stared at the white broken and straight lines on the highway, the exit markers, the lampposts which jutted into the air like the ominous hands of clocks. It made her carsick to look at them, yet she couldn't stop staring.

Only once did they halt on the highway, when they were about halfway there, to fill up the tank with gas at a Mobil station. Miranda bought a Coke to relieve her carsickness.

Two hours later, the car pulled up in front of her grandparents' building in New York. As they rode up the confined, stale-smelling elevator which reminded Miranda of the subway, she still felt carsick. Her heart was drumming like a train rattling over the tracks. Would her grandfather be very weak? Would he talk to them? Would the doctor be there? Would he get better?

They stood in front of the brown metal door of apartment 6C with its nameplate, "Mr. and Mrs. Goldsmith," and rang. In the still hall the bell jangled like a fire alarm. Miranda's father opened the door. The familiar smell of her grandfather's pipe, fresh ironing, a fragrance of vanilla, and of the scented geraniums her grandmother grew on the kitchen sill.

Her father laid his hand on her mother's shoulder and led Miranda in. His eyes, usually animated, had dissolved into a fragile, grave expression.

Miranda's grandmother was sitting on the living-room sofa. Quiet. She looked up as Miranda and her mother entered.

"It's too late, Hannah," she said, gazing sorrowfully at her daughter. "He died an hour ago."

"No," Miranda wanted to cry, the way she had last term when her finger was nearly lopped off by the buffing machine in Jewelry Shop. "No," she wanted to cry with pain. Yet, at the same time, she said to herself, *I knew, I knew all along. I knew in my bones.*

Where had they been an hour ago? Maybe at the Mobil station. At the very moment her grandfather died, she might have been sipping a Coke. The carsickness welled inside her; her mouth tasted sour. They'd missed seeing him by only one hour. How fast terrible things happened. But could they have come faster? If they hadn't gone on the bicycle ride, if they hadn't dawdled in the potato fields, they would have been there for her father's first phone call. But now it was too late, her grandmother had said so.

Miranda's mother said nothing. She walked straight through the living room, past the leather chair Grandpa had always sat on, and into her parents' bedroom. Miranda followed.

Grandpa was lying on the bed, his feet sticking out slightly from the covers. His eyes were shut, hiding those blue eyes bright and sharp; his features were peaceful as if he were napping on the hammock in the country. But his lips looked thinner and his nose longer against his pale face and deep-set eyes.

Miranda's mother took his hands and held them. Her eyes were brimming with tears. They were deep-set like Grandpa's. Miranda stood at the foot of the bed. She pulled the blanket down to cover her grandfather's feet. His toes were cold to her touch.

Her eyes swung to the wall above the head of the bed. There hung Grandma's and Grandpa's wedding picture taken over forty years ago. Grandma wore a white veil low on her forehead and billowing round her face. She looked so gay and pretty. And Grandpa was young and tall and solemn.

Then Miranda's eyes dropped to the night table alongside the bed. It held a thermometer, a bottle of red medicine, a teaspoon, a glass of water, a jar of pills. Things meant to cure Grandpa. But they had not been able to save him. Miranda bit her lip hard 'til she tasted blood. The cut hurt. *It's crazy*, she thought, *how alive one still is near the dead.*

Grandpa was buried two days later. Sonya came home from Colorado. Relatives that Miranda hadn't seen for years and people she'd never seen came for the funeral, and an old friend of her grandfather's delivered the service, talking about her grandfather as a student, a young man, as a friend. He talked about a man Miranda had never known. She had her own memories. She thought about the baby-sitting grandfather who used to bring her candy, hard on the outside, soft and fruity on the inside, and sing lullabies to her when she was little, and invent funny rhymes, and imitate a rooster crowing—*kook-a-ra-koo*—and his childhood pet goat bleating—*ma-maah, ma-maah*—and who was picking beach plums with her only last summer.

The day after the funeral, Sonya returned to classes in Colorado. And Grandma moved into Sonya's old room.

THREE

For most people the New Year begins on January first. For Miranda every year seemed to start on the Monday after Labor Day, the first day of school. Everything was new, like a fresh blank notebook waiting to be filled. Classes, teachers, new friends at school.

But this year it was as if all the lines in the notebook had gone squiggly. Everything had begun on the wrong foot, and wrongest of all was the awful gap left in their lives. Grandpa was gone. Miranda just plain missed him, knowing that he would never come back, or crow like a rooster.

It was a deep ache that she felt at his absence. Somehow it was worse in the morning when she woke up and suddenly remembered all over again that Grandpa was gone. Every night before she fell asleep she thought of him and could see him. She missed his silly rhymes. *All the monkeys in the zoo, they will say hello to you* . . . She missed seeing him approach from the distance with the familiar newspaper rolled under his arm. She missed their games of chess—he was the one who had taught her and at the beginning would sometimes let her win, but then as her skill grew, he played his best.

Sometimes Miranda had the feeling he had simply gone down for the New York *Times* and would return shortly. It was hard to realize that she could not pick up the phone, dial his number and hear that familiar voice of his, rejoicing with her over some good news, or commiserating with her over the bad. He'd always made her feel strong.

Miranda knew that her mother and father missed him too. But they didn't talk about it. For some things, it seemed, people couldn't find words. Why didn't they try? Only this morning, she had come upon her mother, standing by the window, looking out, and when her mother turned at Miranda's footsteps her eyes were bright as though with tears. Miranda wanted to cry out, "Oh, Mommy, don't you miss Grandpa?" But the words didn't come. Instead, she heard herself say, "Did you sleep well?" And her mother's tears, they didn't come, either.

Had Miranda been superstitious, which she wasn't (she never even said "God bless you" when people sneezed), she would definitely have thought of the terrible event as an omen of everything in her life being wrong. One thing after another. Superstitions aside, that's what she secretly believed, anyway.

Take yesterday, for example. Family friends had come to the house to offer condolences, but Miranda felt so tight in her chest, her breath trapped inside, that she had to escape. So she slipped out of the house, took her bicycle from the hall, and headed for the park. She pedaled fast, as fast as she could, even on the steep hill descending to the promenade. Then, suddenly, toward the bottom of the hill she saw a fallen branch on the path. The bicycle was going so fast there was no way to brake. The world tilted and Miranda toppled off. It was a strange fall. Her entire body landed on her left hand. The middle finger began to throb, but Miranda could bend it, which meant the finger wasn't broken. She scrambled to her feet quickly so that no one could see her sprawled on the ground. How humiliating at her age to lose control of her bicycle. But instead of returning home to put ice on the swelling, she rode on. She was headed for a particular place.

About five minutes later she arrived—at the boat basin of Riverside Park. She went directly to a particular bench. *Their bench.* Where she and Grandpa used to sit, and look at the boats, and sometimes read. Where she remembered him reading to her a book he'd given her for her fourth birthday, *The Pirate Twins.* It was about a little girl who one morning discovers a pair of pirate twins washed up on shore who become her friends. At the end of the story the pirate twins vanish, but the little girl always remembers them and waits for them. Somehow, the boat basin with its anchored sloops, the freight boats passing on the Hudson, loaded with construction materials, the Circle Line gliding around the island of Manhattan with tourists, and that first book, *The Pirate Twins,* were strong links between Miranda and Grandpa. Down here she felt close to him. If only he would come back, she was willing to wait a long time.

As Miranda sat, a mother passed, pushing a little boy in his stroller. The child was having a temper tantrum: his arms and legs were stiff with rage and he was screaming at the top of his lungs. When his mother gave him a cookie he threw it to the ground, screaming even louder as she desperately tried to calm him.

Miranda remembered once when she was very

little, she and Grandpa had come down here to the boat basin, and Miranda had insisted that she wanted to go to the zoo, but Grandpa said that it was too late, the zoo would be closing, they'd go tomorrow. She, however, would not believe him and grew angry and ran off as fast as she could 'til she was out of sight. Then she crouched behind a bush and later wandered around the park for hours before wending her way home. When she got there, she found her mother and her sister, terribly worried, while Grandpa and her father were out hunting for her. The police had been notified. When her father and grandfather came home, her father scolded her, but her grandfather was so relieved, he only picked her up and kissed her, and the next day he took her to the zoo.

Miranda began to cry. How guilty she felt for having upset him so. She looked out at the rocky palisades on the opposite shore and at the boats passing on the river and let herself cry freely.

When she opened the front door with her key, she noticed a deep patch of black at the base of the nail on her middle finger. It was like a badge of mourning, similar to the black armbands she'd seen other people in mourning wear. It was *her* badge of mourning. Secretly she was glad it was there.

Yes, her life this September was in a total

muddle. Starting with the smallest things. Last year's shoes didn't fit, and in the confusion of their homecoming, her mother naturally hadn't had time to shop with her for new ones. Miranda couldn't even wear her sneakers because those had been left behind in the country. So on the first day of school, she made her grand appearance in rubber beach thongs!

There were other things she'd left in the country: that half-finished mystery which for some reason stuck in her mind and for which she'd already invented six possible endings, the cream for her pimples, and most important of all, her nonallergic pillow. So now she was sleeping on an old feather pillow and sneezing her fool head off all night long because her mother hadn't found time either to buy her another nonallergic pillow. Not that Miranda blamed her: she had other things on her mind.

From snatches of overheard conversations and observation, Miranda knew everything that her mother had had to attend to in the last couple of days. Such painful details as choosing Grandpa's casket—plain and simple pine it had been—ordering flowers for his funeral—white frilled chrysanthemums and baby's breath. Miranda would have chosen dogwood, his favorite flower, but dogwood was out of season.

Miranda realized how hard it was for her

mother. Yet, strangely, at the funeral service, though her expression was bereft, she had not cried. She was mute. Her face was gray, her eyes so deep-set and blazing in their sockets that it frightened Miranda. It was as if she were looking deep inside herself, maybe into her childhood, and nobody could follow her there. Nobody could share that with her, not even Miranda's father who was holding her arm. Then, before the casket was closed and carried to the burial grounds, her mother had slipped something inside, a sheet of paper. Miranda wondered what was on it. She dared not ask.

And now, her mother was busy, busy as always, busier than ever, organizing the household, making things comfortable for Grandma. Already she'd installed a little radio on the night table so that Grandma could have music and had provided her with an extra pillow. Grandma always slept on two. It was as if Miranda's mother was trying to anticipate Grandma's every need.

Last night, when she saw Grandma sitting quietly in the living room, hands folded on her lap, shoulders bent, her body enveloped in grief, Miranda's mother had said, "Are you okay, Mama? Can I make you a cup of tea?" And she had to repeat it before Grandma raised her head slowly and focused her eyes upon the people around her. "Yes, Hannah, I'm all right." Then Dad went over and took her hand.

In the evening Miranda noticed that though Grandma had a book on her lap, her eyes gazed beyond the print on the page. As if focusing on images and memories of the past. Maybe the words in the book triggered off these memories, or maybe the book served only as a disguise to the others, to make them believe that she was distracted, not suffering. To ease it for them.

When, Miranda wondered, did her grandmother feel loneliest? In the morning when she awoke, or in bed at night? She must feel so alone without Grandpa. Did she dream about him?

But Miranda knew that Grandpa's presence was among them. She had felt it at the dinner table last night, for example, when parsnips were served. Parsnips were Grandpa's favorite vegetable. Or yesterday, when her father took the chess set out of the drawer, opened his mouth as if to invite someone to play, and then laid it back. Grandpa had been his strongest opponent.

But, despite everything, everyone had to go back to their old routines. Miranda to school, her father and mother back to work, her mother to her library. Miranda could tell how badly her mother felt leaving Grandma alone. Before she left in the morning she'd squeeze a tall glass of orange juice for Grandma and set it on her night table, leave the morning newspaper for her, and tell her all sorts of things she could have for lunch. Unlike old times, Grandma lingered in bed as if she were in no hurry to start the day alone. Miranda's mother sensed this and tried to help her fill it. It was as if she had become Grandma's mother, as if Grandma had been orphaned by Grandpa's death. No, Miranda knew that her mother's mind was not on buying shoes. Nor on library aquisitions.

School was no consolation for Miranda. Her program couldn't be grimmer. She had the strictest English teacher in the school, one who assigned a composition every week, handed out a reading list a mile long and who only liked the boys; the same Spanish teacher she'd had for two years in a row, and they were both good and sick of each other; and a homeroom filled with every clown in her grade. Miranda was so disheartened, she didn't even bother buying new clean notebooks, separators, or bright yellow unsharpened number-one pencils with the soft lovely lead. She just didn't care.

What made matters worse, and she felt ashamed to admit such mean thoughts, was being stuck in her old room. In her summer plans she had already moved. This was like being left back or getting ready to go on a trip and then being told at the last minute, "No."

Their family once more—or still—was four. Grandma had replaced Sonya. And Miranda could see herself cooped up forever in that cubby hole. Dressed in a ratty outgrown bathrobe with frayed sleeves.

After the second week of school, she sat in her room, glumly staring at her apple-green dresser, the lopsided rocking chair, inhaling a vague camphor smell. The room looked tinier and dingier than ever. Summer dust covered her books; soot clogged the gauzy white curtains; the begonia plant's bloated leaves drooped from the watering zeal of the neighbor who'd tended the plants during the summer. Out her window the courtyard looked bleak and deserted.

Miranda glared at the stuffed toys, the Raggedy Ann, the teddy bear, all stupidly perched on the top shelf of her bookcase, at the Monopoly set on the second shelf, at the stack of *National Geographics* on the bottom, and finally at her open desk, a jumble of last term's notes, exams, empty candy wrappers, a pin cushion, a torn tube of Elmer's Glue. She ran her fingers through her hair, an old habit of hers, and made faces at the mess.

The muffled sounds of a Pete Seeger record penetrated the wall from the neighbor's apartment. The cheerful music exasperated Miranda, and she felt like banging on the wall, or sticking pins in dopey Raggedy Ann's head.

Tomorrow, Saturday, was cleaning day, but plainly she had to start sorting her things in order to tackle the tons of homework that had already been dished out. With a sigh she plopped down into the chair and began dumping junk into the trash basket, slowly at first, then recklessly. A kind of exhilaration seized her, a fever to get rid of everything. As the desk emptied, the basket filled and overflowed.

Tucked away in one of the cubbies, among pencil stubs, paper clips, and rubber bands, she found an old dog-eared Mary Jane. Absentmindedly she peeled off the sticky wrapper and bit through the hard molasses candy to the peanut butter center. She chewed slowly letting the tip of her tongue wander over the ridges of her palate and lick between her teeth for stray bits of peanut. Suddenly, however, she gulped. Ceased chewing and discarding.

At the bottom of the clutter, faceup, lay two sickeningly familiar books. Library books that she'd taken out last spring for a report on photosynthesis. With a feeling of dread she opened them. According to the cards tucked in the inside pockets, the due date on the books had been May 27.

Today was September 12. Miranda took a pencil and began calculating: the books were 105 days late, not counting Sundays, Memorial Day, or the

Fourth of July. Multiplied by 2, that made 210 days, and multiplying that by a 5¢ penalty produced the impossible sum of $10.50.

She couldn't believe it. Where could she unearth enough money to pay it? Could a minor declare bankruptcy? She felt stupid, careless, helpless, guilty. She, a librarian's daughter! This was the ultimate family dishonor. She could just imagine her mother's stern look. Miranda tried to invent a clever excuse but nothing more original came to mind than a lame "I forgot." She grabbed the books and sent them flying across the room. Then, flinging herself on the bed, she muffled her head into the allergic pillow and began to bawl.

Crying like this was like diving into the waves of the Long Island surf. No sooner did she plunge into one and regain her footing, than along came another to engulf her. Each fresh swell of tears plunged Miranda into the next. She cried and she cried. She cried about the books, about being only thirteen years old, about the same old dreary homework, about her lost room, about Grandpa and the fact that people have to die. As she lay heaving on the bed, she felt a hand touch her. She looked up. It was Grandma.

"Miranda?" She spoke softly. Miranda kept on crying.

Her grandmother did not speak again, but left

her hand on Miranda's shoulder, allowing the out-
burst of tears to run its natural tide. The tide ended
with a crashing sneeze. Miranda raised her head.

Her grandmother handed her a handkerchief.
Miranda blew, but her nose remained stuffy as a
clogged-up drain.

"Is it that bad?" her grandmother asked.

Miranda looked at Grandma's face, made plain
by grief, the eyes shadowed, and she thought of
Grandpa's death, and knew she should say no.

"Yes." Her voice quivered.

"Can I help?"

Miranda shook her head. How could she confide
all her troubles? Confess the disappointment of
losing her coveted room, at the lack of change in
her life, at the impossible library debt—a life's
savings for Miranda, except that her puny life
hadn't accumulated such savings—about her negligence. Thinking of negligence reminded her
abruptly of a note her mother had left on the
kitchen table: "Miranda, at five o'clock put a light
under the baking potatoes for dinner."

"What time is it?" Miranda sniffled, knowing
that this sounded as if she were flippantly changing
the subject.

Her grandmother glanced at the clock on
Miranda's dresser. "Ten past five."

"I'll be right back."

When Miranda returned, she found her grand-mother seated on the bed, holding the library books on her lap and studying the inside pocket. She looked up.

"Is this why you're crying?" she said, pointing to the message that read "Date Due, May 27."

FOUR

The librarian arched one brow higher than the other as she looked at the two way-overdue books. "That will be ten dollars and thirty-five cents," she said.

Miranda, unblinking, handed her two fives and a single bill, wondering why it amounted to fifteen cents less than she expected. The librarian's second brow shot up to meet the first, obviously unprepared for such prompt and full payment. She looked knowingly at Miranda's grandmother.

"It's only a loan," Miranda insisted as they walked down the library steps.

"Only a loan," her grandmother echoed, "a secret loan."

"Grandma, I'll pay you one dollar each week, half of my allowance." Her grandmother nodded.

They began walking up Amsterdam Avenue. As they headed uptown, Miranda realized that their pace was slower than when she walked alone. *Since when does Grandma walk so slow?* she thought. *Is it only since Grandpa's death? Is she walking in slow motion because she's sad, or because she has nowhere to go? Or because she's getting old, maybe sick?* Miranda remembered vaguely many years ago some talk about a heart "condition." *Oh, please, Grandma, don't get sick. Don't . . .*

Deliberately she slowed down and concentrated on measuring her steps to fit her grandmother's. But her feet seemed to have a rhythm of their own, to hurry on. She remembered as a little girl when she walked with her father how hard it had been to keep up with his stride and how sometimes she would get a kink in her side from trying to keep up. Only when she was huffing and puffing did he realize he was walking too fast. Her father was a fast walker, and Miranda took after him.

Though her grandmother walked slow, Miranda could tell that her eyes missed nothing, from the deep gray crevices and fissures in the pavement to the people on Amsterdam Avenue. It was as if she were reemerging, after her great sadness, from her seclusion, doubly sensitized to the everyday world. Miranda remembered having that feeling after having been isolated a long time in the house with the measles or a long cold. Suddenly the world stood out sharp.

A rumpled black man with kinky white hair sat dozing on an old discarded chair in front of a run-down brownstone. On the stoop an elderly couple were chatting, the man in shirtsleeves, suspenders, and straw hat, smoking a cigar, the woman knitting. *Did they intensify Grandma's loneliness?* Miranda wondered. Nearby, a woman with hoop earrings and cheeks the color of her fruit was selling mangos from a wooden crate. From the corner restaurant, marked *El 26 de Enero*, came the smell of fried chicken, *cuchifritos*, and *plátanos*, and the sound of a jukebox blaring a lively Spanish tune. Overhead at an open window, a man was playing his guitar. As Miranda and her grandmother passed, the string broke, its twang vibrating in every nerve. They exchanged glances.

Continuing on, they saw a few paces ahead of them a woman about Grandma's age, all decked out in a veiled hat, white gloves, and a mink jacket, leading on a leash a poodle elegant as its mistress, its white fur clipped into a fancy hairdo. The poodle halted in the middle of the sidewalk, lowered its bottom, and did its business. As

Miranda stepped gingerly around the mess, steering her grandmother to do the same, she saw the owner halt, whip out a little scoop from her purse, shovel up the dog's doings, and dump it in the street.

"Holy toads," Miranda whispered to her grandmother, "all that fuss paid to a dog!" And she began to giggle.

"Some people have little to do with their time," her grandmother replied as they continued behind dog and mistress.

Is she talking about herself? thought Miranda. She knew how heavily Grandpa's absence weighed upon her grandmother.

At the corner, in front of a pizza parlor, a group of boys were squabbling. One in anger threw his pizza at another. The target ducked, and the pizza, instead of landing on the boy's face, like a pie in a Charlie Chaplin movie, landed on the sidewalk. The poodle in front of them strained on its leash, but before it could pull its mistress over, a mangy street dog with a white billy goat beard ran over and gobbled up the pizza.

"Some dogs have all the luck," Grandma said, nudging Miranda, and she laughed. It was the first time Miranda had heard her laugh since before the summer. The walk had done her good. Miranda linked her arm through her grandmother's as they turned the corner and walked toward Broadway.

The tall brick buildings of the West Side rose around them, roofs festooned with rich detail, ornate moldings, cornices carved with creatures and human faces. Weathered green domes and scrollwork interspersed with television aerials ridged the sky.

As they passed the Broadway Cafeteria, her grandmother paused hesitantly. "Shall we go in for a cup of tea?"

Miranda nodded. They pushed through the turnstile, and as each pulled a ticket, a little bell went off. Grandma took a cup of tea in a glass, Miranda took a cup of tea in a cup, and they shared an apple strudel. They sat at a table near the window. Mostly elderly people were in the cafeteria, some in pairs, more of them alone, some reading newspapers, others eating jello, rice pudding, stewed prunes.

From their table, they could watch the passersby on Broadway. A man hurried along, the week's shirts slung on his arm, and entered the Chinese laundry next door to have them washed and starched. Across the street people emerged from the supermarket, rolling laden wagons. A blind man passed, stepping confidently with his cane aloft: his wife walked beside him. An elderly man strolled past, walking with his hands folded behind his back, like Miranda's grandfather used to. Miranda wondered if her grandmother saw him, and if it would make her sad. Miranda felt that familiar tight feeling in her chest. She dropped her eyes.

"Look, Miranda," she heard her grandmother say. "He walks the way Grandpa did."

Miranda looked up and saw Grandma's eyes, gentle with memory. Grateful for hearing her thoughts out loud, grateful to hear the sound of the word *Grandpa*, Miranda smiled and the clogged feeling disappeared. She ran her fingers through her hair and nodded. "He does."

Then suddenly she heard herself saying, "Did Grandpa used to come to this cafeteria?"

Her grandmother stirred the sugar in her tea longer than she had to and looked intently at Miranda.

"How did you know?" she said quietly, and gratefully.

"I just had a feeling."

FIVE

Miranda's mother waved the cake-cutter in the air for emphasis and laid a slice of pumpkin pie in front of her mother. "Mother, you're only sixty-four years old. You look fifty-four. Youth is in the heart. It'll be just like home here. Dad would have wanted it this way, for you to live with us, not to be alone."

Miranda's father agreed. "We have plenty of room. You can come and go as you wish. Our house is your house."

"You're both good to me," said Grandma.

"You ought to start thinking about giving up your apartment. Life will be much simpler for you here. You won't have to worry about taking care of things, laundry, marketing, cleaning, paying rent . . ."

Miranda began swaying on the front legs of her chair, wondering if her mother's life was very difficult. It must be hard for her to fit in everything. But what could she eliminate? Her work, her household tasks, her obligations to Grandma, to her family . . . to Miranda. Everyone counted on her, expected things of her. And she always came through.

Life isn't a picnic, they say. Was it always that complicated to be grown-up? Maybe it was better to be a child. Their next-door neighbor liked to tell Miranda that this was the best time of her life. Maybe she was right. Maybe thirteen years old was a good age to be.

"Miranda, please stop swinging on your chair," her mother put in, interrupting what she'd been saying.

"I wasn't swinging on my chair," Miranda grumbled, unaware that indeed she had been.

Her mother looked at her crookedly and went on. "As I was saying, there's no need for you to have the burden . . . We *want* to have you."

As Miranda continued listening uneasily, she crossed her legs and jiggled the right leg over the left knee. With each jiggle the leg banged the trestle under the table.

Her father turned to her. "Miranda, please stop kicking the table!" She uncrossed her legs and remained poised on the edge of her seat. Why were grownups so nervous, so irritable, about little things? She heard her grandmother speaking.

"I have my social security and your father's now, too. I could afford to keep my apartment...."

"There are so many activities you could do," her mother went on. "At the Y they have an active Senior Citizen's Club with lectures and poetry readings. You can see old movies at the Museum of Modern Art. You and Dad were such movie fans. You can take French lessons at the Alliance Française, as you've always threatened to do, and pottery classes too. Working with clay would be wonderful for the arthritis in your fingers." Miranda's mother spoke with an optimistic tone, as if all possibilities lay ahead. "But the first thing to do is give up your apartment."

Miranda's grandmother rose and started to clear the table. "We'll see," she said.

"Leave all that, Mother. You don't have to clear. I'd like you to take it easy."

"It's all right, Hannah. I want to."

Miranda jumped from her chair, picked up the empty pie plate, and followed her grandmother into the kitchen.

"Grandma, are you really interested in French

and in pottery?" she asked as they loaded the dishwasher together. She was thinking of her own battles with Spanish verb conjugations and couldn't imagine anyone studying a foreign language just for the *fun* of it.

"Well, to tell you the truth, Miranda, at one point Grandpa and I were planning to spend a summer in southern France and talked about taking classes together. That was before your mother was born, before I stopped working at the library. But now . . ."

"And pottery?"

Miranda's grandmother poured some soap into the dishwasher and held up her fingers. "These fingers of mine are knobby and crooked." She made a wry face. "But I'll have to uncrook them in my own way."

They both fell silent and Miranda dawdled around the stove, rummaging around inside herself for some hidden thought that teased like a buzzing fly. In a moment she heard her mother call from the living room. "Miranda, have you finished your homework?" At this reminder, the secret thought burst forth. Why did her mother think she could organize Grandma's life the way she tried to organize Miranda's? As if they were both library books that could be tucked away safely in their proper place on the proper shelf.

Again, Miranda felt that tug to pull away, to run contrary to her mother's plans, battling with the other urge, to stay little Miranda.

"I finished my homework," Miranda called out crossly. "I don't have to be reminded. I'm not a baby."

Grandma looked at her but did not comment. She dried her hands on the kitchen towel and headed for the hall closet. Taking out her coat, she put it on.

"Where are you going?"

"Over to the store to pick up some honey." Grandma always drank hot milk and honey before going to bed. She'd done it since she was a child, she once told Miranda. It helped her fall asleep.

"Can I go with you?"

"Ask your mother."

As Miranda was going in to ask, her mother came out to the hall.

"Mama, you're not going out at this hour, are you?"

"It's only half past seven."

"It's not really safe to walk in the streets of New York at this hour."

"It's only half past seven and the streets are well lit. I've always gone for a walk after dinner."

Miranda knew that she had always gone out with Grandpa. "Mom, please let me go with

Grandma. I'm all finished with my work."

"Well . . . I guess so, but come back soon so that you don't take your bath at all hours of the night."

The September air was soft as the inside of a slipper. Across the street a boy Miranda knew from school whizzed by on his skateboard and shouted hello. Miranda waved back, envying his speed. She looked up at the sky, an oblong sash pinned between the high city buildings, and thought of the wide summer sky seeded with stars as far as you could see. Summer and the country, open space and endless skies, seemed ages ago.

Halfway down the block they ran into Mrs. Polansky, one of Grandma's neighbors.

"Oh, Mrs. Goldsmith," she said, glancing uneasily at Grandma. "I was so sorry to hear about your husband . . ." Her voice trailed off as she nervously kneaded her clenched fists.

"I know," Grandma said gently, as if she were trying to make it easier for the other woman. Miranda took her grandmother's hand as they moved on. The church bells of the Greek Orthodox church a block away chimed eight times.

At Pick 'N Pay, the twenty-four-hour store on Broadway, they bought a jar of honey, and then, the excuse for the walk accomplished, continued to stroll along. They paused at the Riviera moviehouse to study the photographs and the coming attractions. Today *Ninotchka* was playing, with Greta Garbo. A billboard displayed a large close-up of Garbo. She reminded Miranda of a statue of Venus on the ground floor of the Metropolitan Museum of Art. A broad forehead, slender nose, lofty cheekbones, large eyes. Garbo's hair, however, was chin length, while Venus' hair was long. Both Venus and Garbo seemed the essence of womanhood.

Miranda's grandmother gazed at the photos intently, as if they were an album recalling fragments of her own past.

"You know, Miranda, Greta Garbo was your grandfather's favorite actress. When I was younger, I used to be jealous of her. Can you imagine?" She smiled. "But Grandpa loved me to the end of his life. He loved me even more, I think, as we grew older. We understood each other better. He used to call me 'my gray-haired love.' "

It seemed funny to Miranda to think that old people could still talk about love romantically. She half closed her eyes into slits and tried to imagine her grandmother as a young girl. Possibly she had looked like Miranda. People often remarked on the family resemblance. Maybe that was one of the reasons Miranda felt so close to her. Would she look and be like Grandma one day?

As they turned to leave, Miranda cast a parting

glance at Garbo and then noticed that her grandmother was walking over to the box office. For a
moment Miranda had the happy thought that her
grandmother had impulsively decided to buy
tickets for the movies.

"How many please?" the cashier asked, chewing
gum a mile a minute. She was wearing a frizzy
blond wig.

"Uh . . . none, thank you," Grandma said, but
continued to stand there. She was looking at a sign
that read: WANTED. CASHIER. PART TIME. INQUIRE
MANAGER INSIDE.

"Would you please step aside?" said the cashier.
"You're blocking the line." The "line" consisted
of one man waiting to buy a ticket.

Grandma stepped aside long enough for him to
do so, and then asked, "Is the manager here?"

The cashier snapped her gum. "What is this in
reference to?"

"The cashier position," Grandma said. Miranda
looked at her in surprise. The cashier scrutinized
her skeptically, a sneaky smile lurking round her
lips as if to say, "You're too old." Miranda felt
like tearing off her wig.

"He's on his lunch break," the cashier replied,
pursing her lips. *How could anyone be eating lunch
at eight o'clock at night?* Miranda wondered.

Grandma persisted. "When will he be back?"

"He won't be back," said the cashier, her nose twitching. "He has to go to the bank afterwards." It was obviously a lie.

As they turned to leave, a man in a formal black suit, white shirt, and silver-striped tie came up to the box office. He was dressed as if for a wedding. "How are we doing tonight?" he asked the cashier. Miranda saw her wink and signal to Grandma.

Her grandmother marched straight up to the man. "Are you the manager?"

He cleared his throat and tightened his tie. "Yes," he responded in a stuffy tone.

"I'm interested in the cashier vacancy," Grandma said with almost equal formality. Somehow she sounded more like a librarian than a cashier.

The manager expertly cased the elderly woman, dubiously eyeing her gray hair, her old-fashioned oxfords, the pearls around her neck. Miranda felt that he even noticed her knobby arthritic fingers. He cleared his throat again. "Well, I believe the position is filled, but you may leave your name and address if you wish."

He's just trying to get rid of her, Miranda thought. The cashier, with a smug look on her face, handed over pencil and paper, and Grandma wrote down her name, address, and phone number on a slip of paper that looked as if it would get thrown away as soon as their backs were turned.

"Do you really want to work?" Miranda asked her grandmother on the way home.

"I hadn't considered it 'til this moment, but it's an idea. As they say, the days are long, but the years drag by. I'm so used to being with your grandfather. . . . Sometimes I'm afraid I've lost all my force. I've forgotten how it is to lead a life alone."

"But you're not alone, Grandma," said Miranda. "You have us . . . *me*."

Her grandmother squeezed her hand.

At home Miranda's mother had a steaming bath ready for Miranda. Somehow that annoyed Miranda. It was so babyish. At the same time she felt a twinge of guilt for resenting her mother's thoughtfulness.

"Mom, I wish I had hair like Greta Garbo. Short, silky. Not this snarly old seaweed. It's always greasy these days."

"Miranda, what *are* you talking about? Your hair is beautiful, blond, and silky as corn tassels."

Oh, God, thought Miranda, making a dash for the bathroom. *She thinks I look like Alice in Wonderland. Next thing, she'll call it cute, and tie it with a pink satin ribbon.* . . . She slammed the door, locked it, and undressed. In front of the medicine-chest mirror, she sucked in her cheeks and held her hands over the bottom part of her hair. Despite these efforts, her round face and stubby nose looked more like W. C. Fields' than Greta Garbo's. Her head squatted on her shoulders like a turtle's. No neck. Miranda No-Neck. She plunged into the tub and submerged her head in the hot soapy water. A shampoo was the best medicine for anything.

The "medicine" worked better than she expected. It relaxed her so that she nearly dozed off in the tub, but was startled back to reality by her mother banging on the door and shouting, "Miranda, what are you *doing* in there? It's almost eleven o'clock."

Miranda, damp and flushed, stumbled from the steamy bathroom into bed, vaguely remorseful about not brushing her teeth or saying good night to Grandma.

It was worth going to sleep—her dreams were blissful. One strung after another like a paper chain. She was sitting in a vast Long Island field of bright green winter wheat and looking out toward the dunes, her hair short and blowing free. And then there was another dream. She was skating in an enormous room with a domed ceiling and arches all around, and the floor had large black-and-white squares, like a hopscotch pattern . . . But suddenly, reluctantly, Miranda woke up.

She sat up in bed. What was it that had awakened her? It was very still in the house. The hands of her alarm clock glowed in the dark. Twenty past two. The shade flapped at the window and pale fingers of light crept under. Suddenly Miranda heard a cry, like the one, she realized, that had awakened her.

She climbed out of bed and tiptoed across the cold floor to the next room. Her grandmother was snoring quietly. Her arms were flung back over her head in a childlike pose. The patchwork quilt she'd brought from her own place was bundled round her. It was a quilt Miranda remembered her working on for a long time, made of diamond-shaped pieces, many of them remnants of dresses Grandma had stitched through the years for Miranda and her sister.

Miranda felt uneasy looking at her grandmother in her sleep. It seemed wrong to be spying on someone in an unguarded moment. She patted the quilt and turned to go back to her room. But as she did, the cry came again. It was Grandma calling "Mama" in her sleep.

Miranda didn't turn on the light. She turned away and left Grandma with her dreams.

SIX

"It's for you, Mother. Telephone."

Miranda awoke to the sound of her mother thumping on Grandma's door. Saturday morning, the one day Miranda could sleep late. No classes, no Sunday School. No peace.

Miranda came to the breakfast table, sullen.

"What's come over you lately, Miranda?" her mother asked.

Miranda poured herself some Rice Krispies and stuck the cereal box in front of her face.

Her grandmother walked in. She was all dressed, especially neat. Ready to go out.

"Good morning, everybody," she said.

"Who phoned you so early?" Miranda's mother

asked. And before an answer was made, "And where are you going?" She sounded so nosy, thought Miranda, though she must admit, she herself was kind of curious.

"To work," Grandma answered.

"What?" Miranda's mother held the percolator in mid-air, as shocked as if Grandma had announced she was going to hold up a bank.

"Yes," Grandma nodded. "The manager of the Riviera called to offer me a job. I start in half an hour. They're having a kiddy show, and another cashier that they hired quit before she began."

"The Riviera? What are you talking about?" Miranda's mother demanded. Just then her father came into the kitchen.

"What's this I hear about the Riviera?" He bent over and kissed Miranda on the head. "Miranda, are you going off to the sunny Riviera?" He laughed. Dad was the best audience for his own jokes.

"I wish I were," Miranda replied glumly.

"No, I am, Michael. I have a job as a cashier at the Riviera Theatre."

"I can't believe it, Mother. You must be fooling. You wouldn't work as a *cashier*, out on the sidewalk, exposed to full view! It's not right, it's . . ."

Miranda mentally finished her mother's sentence —*it's below you.*

Grandma smiled. "Oh, Hannah, don't be such a snob."

Miranda bit her lips to hold back her approval.

"It's not that, Mother. But you haven't worked in years."

"Don't you think I can do it, Hannah?"

"It's not that, but you're too . . ." She broke off.

"Too old?" Grandma finished. *Glory, glory!* Miranda sang inside. Her grandmother sure knew how to say things straight out.

"No, that's *not* what I was going to say. I was going to say, you're too qualified."

"Qualified for what? Pottery classes, French lessons, senior citizens' socials?"

"You know that's not what I mean. You're a librarian, like I am."

"Hannah, how old are you?" Grandma asked.

"Thirty-nine."

"Well, I haven't been a librarian for thirty-nine years. I stopped being a librarian a month before you were born. I don't even remember the Dewey decimal system."

Miranda smiled happily. Neither did she.

"There's no reason why I can't get you a volunteer job at our library. We always need extra help."

"I don't want a volunteer job, Hannah, and I don't need you to get me a job at your library," Grandma said quietly. "Look, we'll talk later. I have to leave or I'll be late."

"Without tea?" Miranda asked. Tea was Grandma's staff of life. Darjeeling tea.

"Don't worry, Miranda. I'll have some later."

"I still don't think it's safe. You hear such stories these days . . . and read such terrible headlines." Miranda's mother looked anxious, as if she wanted to cling to her mother.

"Don't worry, Hannah dear," Grandma repeated. "I can take care of myself."

"When will you be back?" Miranda's mother stirred her spoon round and round in her cup.

"I don't know. Later. Good-bye, everybody."

"I can't believe it," Miranda's mother said after the front door closed.

"What's so terrible about Grandma taking a job?" Miranda asked. "*You* work."

"Imagine her sitting in that cage all day. And my friends passing by and seeing her."

So that is it, thought Miranda. Her mother, in addition to everything, didn't want Grandma to be on public display. To take what *she* considered a lowly job. Miranda wondered if her mother feared that one day *she* might be reduced to being a cashier. What would happen if Miranda announced that she was going to be one? It was less boring than being a tollbooth taker or an elevator operator. In fact, come to think of it, it was *interesting*. Watching the stream of people go by, observing the scene.

"It's certainly something *I'd* never do." her mother went on.

Miranda gloated inwardly at her correct guess. "I don't see anything wrong with Grandma taking that job."

"Oh, Miranda, you wouldn't understand! You're too young!"

Miranda *knew* she'd say that.

"I'm not too young to know that Grandma has a right to lead her own life," she shot back. And she felt like adding, "And me too!"

"What is this, Miranda, are you and your grandmother in cahoots?" her father put in. "Your mother is right. It isn't safe."

"Or . . . or proper," his wife concluded.

"Let's drop it now," said Miranda's father. "We'll discuss it when Grandma gets back."

Miranda stood up from the table. She knew they'd discuss it more when she was out of earshot. They thought she was too childish, too immature, to take into their confidence. Sometimes she had the feeling they saved *really* important matters for private discussion. After all, what value did her opinion have?

"Miranda, what are you doing today?" her mother asked.

"Jenny and I are going to the movies. They're playing *Bride of Frankenstein* at the Globe. Can I have my allowance?"

"Wouldn't you rather go the the Cloisters with Daddy and me? They're having a special exhibit of medieval tapestries."

Miranda fidgeted. "Sorry, Mom, I already made this date with Jenny." Her mother knew how she hated museums, loathed them, despised them, detested them. She knew that all those paintings and mummies were uplifting, but . . . She excused herself and went into her room and did six fast push-ups and stood on her head.

SEVEN

Miranda stationed herself across the street from the Riviera to watch her grandmother in action. A line of noisy kids was crowding in front of the cashier's box while Grandma, inside the little booth, was taking money, giving change, tearing off tickets, answering the telephone. She seemed a trifle flustered as the kids bumped and jostled each other, but she was managing. Miranda felt proud of her, as if her grandmother had gone public.

Grandma now seemed doubly precious for those private moments they'd been sharing in the last month and a half. She was such a comfort to Miranda. You could tell her anything, even secrets.

She was never a judge, though she had her own opinions and expressed them freely. She was one person who could come out and say what she felt. How Miranda admired that.

But best of all was that leisurely sense of time you had when you were with her. She was never hurried or impatient. Her schedule wasn't crowded like . . . Miranda cut herself short for the disloyal thought nudging her. After all, her mother had her own life to lead and did things with Miranda that Grandma didn't—hiking, collecting shells by the sea, picking mussels, water coloring. But still, Miranda did treasure those quiet times with Grandma, winding wool with her, airing their pillows on the windowsill in the morning, following some of Grandma's old-fashioned cures, like steaming over a hot kettle—a dual remedy for pimples and allergies. Grandma would speak about the little village in Poland where she had grown up, and the black mushrooms she'd picked in the forest, and how she used to play jacks with little pebbles and skinny-dip in an icy pond in the woods. Somehow, since Grandpa's death, memories of her childhood had surged in her mind and it seemed to ease her spirit to share them with young Miranda. It was like airing the pillows. Yes, Miranda and her grandmother were very close to each other these days.

Miranda leaned against a lamppost and looked at her grandmother. *I knew she could do it,* she said to herself. Then to while away the time 'til her grandmother was free, she watched the passersby. She knew plenty of neighborhood characters, the shabby man seated across the way who sat on the island of benches everyday and ate a roll from a paper bag, the elderly woman wearing a pince-nez who fed bread crumbs to the piegons . . . But most of the people who passed, she didn't know. To think she'd lived in New York all her life, and in this neighborhood, and on one block, yet still didn't know everyone, or even almost everyone. The city was so vast and anonymous. She sighed and glanced across the street for the familiar face inside the box office. Grandma was still busy.

Miranda turned and gazed idly into the shop window. It was one of the oldest stores in the neighborhood. They rented tuxedos. Two mannequins, a bride and groom, stood in the window, smiling in eternal wedding bliss. A sign said: YOU GET MARRIED ONLY ONCE. WHY BUY A TUXEDO? RENT. Next door to the tuxedo rental was a beauty parlor. Three disembodied heads gaped at the sidewalk, one wearing a black wig, another a red wig, the third, a blond. Their reflections were caught in a rear window. A sign in the window read: WE SPECIALIZE IN LONG HAIR. *That means me,* thought Miranda, and she studied herself in the mirror. Her hair, despite last night's shampoo, looked greasy and straggly.

In the mirror she caught herself making faces. She began fingering the allowance that had been given her that morning. Half of the money was reserved, the weekly installment on her library loan from Grandma. She about-faced toward the Riviera. But this time it was not only Grandma and the Riviera she saw. Soaring above the building, like a radiant mirage, was Greta. Dear Greta Garbo! With ethereal free hair . . . A symbol of womanhood, of independence.

The decision no longer rested in Miranda's power. Her feet on their own floated into the beauty parlor. Fumes of lotions, hair spray, shampoo, creams, ammonia, other unidentifiable odors, drifted forth. The place was humid and musky as a dense underbrush. A low hum of women's voices formed the background, like twittering birds when you enter a clearing in the woods. A voice in a pink uniform stepped forward.

"May I help you?"

Peering past the pink uniform into the parlor, Miranda viewed a row of seated women, heads bound in rollers, seemingly attached to the domed dryers overhead. Miranda pushed her hair behind her ears, swallowed, and said casually, "How much is a haircut, please?"

The magic words set gears in motion. Miranda

was instantly turned over to another pink uniform, a young, brisk beautician with a cropped head.

"Step up, miss," she said, guiding Miranda into a high leather chair.

Miranda, facing the mirror, pulled her skirt over her knees the way she did at the dentist's, and stared at herself. Her sidewalk assurance had deserted her, and a froglike woebegone look made her eyes seem twice their natural size. A white length of gauze was wound round her neck; she felt like a mummy being prepared for funeral rites. Then a green plastic cape fell over her shoulders, leaving the head exposed as a target. Miranda closed her eyes a moment to resuscitate Garbo's image.

"How short would you like it?" the beautician asked.

Miranda inserted a length of front hair between her middle and index fingers. The young woman nodded and in a wink had made a wide decisive first snip. Her fingers moved quick as a sleight-of-hand magician.

Miranda was in the chair only ten minutes. In those ten minutes her hair was halved. The beautician stood back and surveyed Miranda's head, scissors still snipping the air. She looked as if she could go on forever. Miranda was a hairdresser's dream.

"Would you like me to take off a smidge more?" she asked hopefully.

Miranda gazed at herself in the mirror. Her new self. Her hair was chin length, like Garbo's, and her neck rose straight as a column, where before it had jutted out squat as a turtle's. The straggly ends were gone; the bottom was straight as an arrow.

"Would you?" the beautician repeated. "A *little* more?"

Miranda glanced at the floor, at the peacock fan of hair, *her* hair, that encircled the chair, and then looked sideways at the beautician's cropped head.

"I think that will be enough," she said in the polite but firm tone of someone refusing second helpings.

She looked beautiful. Suddenly she had a neck, visible, exposed, a proper resting place for her head. Miranda practiced a little smile in the mirror. Without all that hair, her features seemed more expressive. She was more herself!

All her doubts and hesitations were gone. She couldn't believe how easy it was to cut, to remove, to change—once you made up your mind. She'd never had a haircut in her life. Can you imagine? Thirteen years old and still sporting the original mat she'd been born with—plus. It was primitive. Her mother had always regarded Miranda's hair as her best feature. But for Miranda, the long hair was a vestige of babyhood; Goldilocks, curly locks, to please mama, the epitome of Shirley Temple rather than Greta Garbo.

"Would you like to take it home with you?" the beautician asked, like a waiter offering a doggie bag.

"What for?" asked Miranda, glad to be rid of it.

"I don't know. Some people save their hair . . ." The young woman smiled lamely as she rang up the money in the cash register.

Miranda, the new Miranda, sister of Garbo, sailed into the street. She felt inches taller. She was a long-stemmed rose. A drum majorette high-stepping down Broadway, toes first, arms swinging, head bobbing with little airs and graces. Suddenly the day had wings. If it was that easy to change her hair, why not other things, too?

Head elevated like a swan's, she smiled at the mannequins in the tuxedo rental shop and then crossed Broadway. She nodded in a queenly manner to the man with the roll, the woman feeding the pigeons, and to the pigeons themselves. Was everyone noticing how different she was?

The sky was a cloudless luminous blue, a banner for her new sense of freedom. As she strode home, the breeze from the river stroked her neck.

EIGHT

When her grandmother came home two hours
later, she found Miranda relaxed as a rag doll on
the living room chaise, stirring from a nap. After
admiring Miranda's haircut, she brewed them a
pot of tea, and over tea and Fig Newtons, told
Miranda about *her* first haircut, when she'd arrived from Europe, long of hair but short of cash.
How she'd sold her hair for ten dollars to a beauty
parlor on Madison Avenue and bought a red
blouse with the money, a red blouse with a tasseled
belt. She smiled at the memory.

Grandma had lots to talk about. Her head
bobbed like a top as she described her busy morning at the theatre. Sometimes Miranda forgot she

was sixty-four. Miranda thought of the wedding picture of Grandma and Grandpa—how young Grandma had looked then—of the snapshots kept in the top drawer of Grandpa's bureau—there was even a baby picture of Grandma there—and of how Grandma slept with her arms thrown back, like a litle girl. First you're young, then you're less young, and gradually you grow old and then older. A woman is the child she was—plus.

When her mother came home alone, for her father had gone on an errand, Miranda and Grandma were playing gin rummy, and Miranda was giggling as Grandma imitated Mr. Castleway saying "Standing room only."

"Miranda, what have you done to your head?" her mother cried out in the doorway.

"I didn't do anything to my *head*. I cut my hair," Miranda said, stroking the even ends.

"How *could* you? Your beautiful hair!" Miranda ground her teeth, waiting for her mother to launch into corn tassel talk.

"It's *my* hair," said Miranda, slumping in her chair. And she felt like adding, not your damn precious treasure. What was she saving it for? Miranda should have accepted the beautician's offer and brought it home for her mother. A keepsake of her little girl.

"You did it against my wishes. *That's* why you

didn't want to go to the museum. You had it planned."

They glared at each other in silence, Miranda angry at the false accusation, her mother helpless to bring back the lost hair. *This is an act of rebellion, the end of an era,* decided Miranda.

"Hannah," put in Grandma, breaking the silence, "don't be so upset. Hair grows back."

Miranda bit the inside of her cheek. "I don't *want* it to grow back."

"But it *can* grow back," Grandma said. "And maybe at some point you'll want it to grow back. Who knows? Change is good. Miranda can always . . ."

"Mother, I didn't ask for your opinion." She pursed her lips. "Let's change the subject. What else did you do today, Miranda?" Her voice was strained, the way it was when she tried to avoid annoying topics. Miranda didn't answer. Her mother turned to Grandma. "And how about you, Mother, how was your job?"

"Confusing," Grandma admitted. "I felt I needed two more hands. But somehow I managed. The money checked out correctly. And a little boy gave me a frozen Milky Way because he said I reminded him of Mary Poppins. In fact, I have to go back again this evening. I'm doing the night shift also."

"What? Working at night? Mama, I really don't think it's sensible for you to be walking home late at night alone. The city isn't safe. People get hurt." Her daughter spoke urgently. "We have to protect you."

"Hannah, I know your intentions are good. But I can't live in a tangle of memories. I don't want my years ahead to be wasted, dependent. You'll kill me with kindness. Sometimes people have to take risks." Miranda felt as if Grandma were speaking for both of them.

"It isn't a good idea," her daughter insisted.

"Today's the only day I'll be doing it. The manager asked me to do him a favor. They're planning to hire another woman. I promised. I want to be useful."

Miranda jumped up. "Mom, let me go with Grandma. Tomorrow's Sunday. No school. I can watch the movie while she works, and then we'll come home together."

She watched her mother glance across the table, studying her intently, her short hair, her eyes, her uptilted chin. And then her mother's gaze shifted to Grandma, as if comparing the two, linking the two. Suddenly Miranda saw herself in her mother's position, grown-up, wanting to help her daughter and her mother, to please them, yet to protect them.

"Mother, please," she said softly. "We'll be

careful. We'll walk on the bright side of the street."

Her mother stood up, walked over to Miranda, and wound her arm around Miranda's shoulder. "Well, I guess two walking are better than one . . . Miranda, I'm sorry I was such a schoolmarm about your hair. To tell the truth, the haircut does become you. You look different, though. I'll have to get used to it."

Miranda felt exhilarated. "I am different, I am different," she wanted to shout. One giant step forward had been made, like in that children's game, "Mother, May I?"

"Oh, by the way," her mother went on. "There's a letter from Sonya. I left it on the hall table. She's enjoying school, says Colorado is beautiful. I'm glad she's happy, but . . . to tell the truth, I miss her."

Miranda cupped her hand in her chin and gazed at her mother with a new sympathy. How come it had never occurred to her? *She misses Sonya. She misses Grandpa. That makes her want to hold on to me and Grandma, even though she has so much to fill her time. Being busy in your day is one thing, feeling lonely, separated, is another.* After all, her mother, too, had to ease her way into changes.

After dinner, as she and her grandmother stood in the hall waiting for the elevator, her grandmother turned to her. "What do you think, Miranda? Do you think I can do it? Am I still capable of holding a job? I wonder what Grandpa would advise."

Miranda broke in. "Of course you can do it, Grandma. I've seen you do it. And it'll get easier as you go along."

Her grandmother tilted her head, uncertain, but Miranda's enthusiasm was contagious and she smiled gently. "You do look different."

Miranda looked at herself in the hall mirror. Did she really look different? She tucked her hair behind her ears and studied herself. It sounded funny, but her ears were her best feature: close to her head, small earlobes, and attached. Not like her sister, poor thing, whose lobes dangled loose like a monkey's. As soon as the haircut storm blew over completely, Miranda decided she'd have holes pierced in her ears so that she could wear earrings all the time. Little gold loops. Lots of girls in school had done it. But she could predict her mother's reaction: "Punching holes in your ears. What a barbaric custom!" Was that the real reason her mother objected, or was it another way of resisting Miranda's growing up?

Miranda turned to her grandmother. "Grandma, let me see your ears."

Her grandmother eyed her curiously. "My ears?"

"Yes," said Miranda, and she reached for her grandmother's face and pulled her closer.

"Mm-hmmph. That's what I thought. We both have them attached. I know I got them from you. I learned in biology that they're inherited. Thank you, Grandma, thank you!" She squeezed her grandmother's earlobe; she was feeling so silly, so giddy, and so good! They both broke into laughter.

"Yes, Miranda, we have a lot in common. We're both at a crossroads."

NINE

Stuffy Mr. Castleway turned out to be a sweetheart. Not only did he allow Miranda to enter the movies free, but he even treated her to a bag of buttered popcorn. Miranda sat happily in the dark, chewing the kernels slowly to make them last longer.

The theatre had a special smell, confined, warm, protective. It was dreamlike, removed from the real world. At last the images flickered on the great white screen. The show was on. The Moment had arrived: Miranda Stone meets Greta Garbo. *Ninotchka*, an old lighthearted movie, was a sort of fairy tale, but with a complicated plot involving Soviet emissaries, a spy, the theft of crown jewels. Miranda soon stopped bothering to follow the plot and lavished her undivided attention on Garbo. Tall, willowy, radiant, spiritual. And, to top it off, she spoke with an intriguing foreign accent.

It was the first time Miranda had gone to the movies alone, and she was glad that no one was there to whisper, giggle, or otherwise interrupt her private fantasies. At The End, she floated out with the audience, illusions intact. Her grandmother was waiting for her in the lobby.

"I checked out perfectly again tonight," she told Miranda. "Mr. Castleway says he's *most* pleased with me, and my job is permanent."

Miranda had to jolt herself back to reality. As she congratulated her grandmother, she heard a slight Garbo accent in her own speech. Grandma was as excited as a kid with a first job. It set Miranda wondering how soon she too would be able to get a job. Real work that she was paid for, and not simply chores and favors.

Why, if she studied the Want Ads she could probably come up with plenty of jobs she was competent to do. If only grown-ups would believe it. She could answer a switchboard, be a guide in Rockefeller Center—she knew the ins and outs of that place so well—she could run an elevator, be a carpenter's assistant, she could walk dogs . . . Why, the list was endless. She could even be a librarian's assistant! These thoughts turned her mind to money.

"You know, Grandma," she said, "I'm sorry, but I won't be able to pay you this week's installment on my loan because I spent all my money on my haircut. But next week I can give you one dollar."

"Don't worry, Miranda. You credit is good. Anyhow, I'm twelve dollars richer tonight." She held up her handbag and waved it triumphantly like a boxer waving his mitt. "The first money I've earned in thirty years." Her face glowed. "Come, I'll treat you to an ice-cream soda."

When they reached home, all the lights were off, except for the lamp in the living room. Grandma kissed Miranda goodnight, went to her room, and a few minutes later, Miranda could hear music coming from her radio. Miranda's mother was right. Music was such a comfort. Miranda suddenly felt an urge to tell her mother about the movie, and ask how old you had to be to get working papers, and if she knew anyone who was looking for a thirteen-year-old who could do lots of things.

She walked down the hallway and knocked at her parents' door. She knew that tonight her father was out, attending a meeting. It was not that late; her mother was probably reading. Miranda knocked.

Her mother didn't answer, but Miranda knew she was there. A sliver of light cut through the chink of the door. Maybe her mother had fallen asleep over her book: she sometimes did that. Miranda would slip the reading glasses off her mother's nose, insert the bookmark on the open page, and lay the book on the night table. She'd done it often.

Quietly she opened the door so as not to disturb her mother's sleep. Her eyes swept to the bed. The bed was empty. The closet door was open. Her mother was standing halfway inside it, back turned to Miranda. She did not hear Miranda enter. She was strangely still. Not rummaging for a night-gown and slippers, not hanging up anything. Miranda approached.

"Mom . . ."

Her mother swung around, as if jolted from a revery. In her hand she held a pair of pajamas. Men's pajamas, striped white and blue. Miranda recognized them at once. They were the pajamas Grandpa used to wear years ago when he slept over to baby-sit for Miranda. Her mother's face was twisted with grief. *She must have just come across them*, thought Miranda. She stooped and picked up a belt that had fallen and rolled it nervously in her hands.

"Mom, I came to say goodnight . . ." Miranda

felt uneasy to have caught her mother in this private moment. Her mother would feel humiliated, caught off guard, like Miranda felt when she fell off the bicycle. Her mother was always strong, cheerful, protective of those around her, helping to make life easier for the others, from the smallest details to the larger ones. And here she was, alone, closeting her grief. Had she known that Grandpa's pajamas were still hung here? Had she held on to them like a physical remnant of Grandpa's existence? "Mother, are you okay?" Miranda heard herself say. Her mother looked at her, the way Grandma had looked at *her* daughter when asked the same question in the days after Grandpa's death.

Miranda could see tears welling up in her mother's eyes, but they were held back. Come to think of it, Miranda had never seen her mother cry. She knew that her mother wanted to cry, but couldn't. How old had she been when she learned to conceal her feelings, not to utter feelings too painful to express? How hard it must have been for her these past months to help Grandma and to keep things going, despite her own suffering. *It's hard to be the strong one. People grow to expect it of you, to think it comes effortlessly.* Miranda took her mother's hand. She felt it quiver under her touch. A fierce quiet enveloped the room.

Surely her mother could hear Miranda's heart throbbing.

"Oh, Mom, isn't it hard to be without Grandpa?"

Her mother's hand tightened so hard that it nearly hurt Miranda. Miranda took her mother's hand and kissed it. A tear fell upon the hand. *Mine? Hers?* Miranda said nothing. Then her mother looked Miranda full in the face. And the veil that had held the tears back lifted and tears began to drop, separate at first, and then in a stream.

"Oh, my father, my father's gone!"

Miranda did not speak. She held her mother and let her cry. As if one, they moved to the bed and sat down. In a while, her mother's crying subsided. She sat with the pajamas on her lap.

"I never cry," she said to Miranda.

"Well, I do," said Miranda.

"I never cry," her mother repeated.

"Mom, what was it that you wrote on the slip of paper you laid beside Grandpa?"

Her mother looked at her.

"It was a poem, a lullaby he used to sing to me when I was a little girl, the one he used to sing to you." Again her eyes filled with tears, and suddenly Miranda felt the words of that lullaby she knew so well rise inside her and sing themselves:

By my child's cradle at night,
Sleeps her goat so snowy white.
Off the goat goes to market,
Precious child, do not weep,
Soon we'll have raisins and almonds,
Sleep, my little one, sleep.

As she sang, Miranda could imagine her mother as a child, and she felt herself leap forward into the future, could see herself as a woman, a mother, and her own mother as a grandmother. They were all linked. And Grandpa was linked to each of them in a different way: husband, father, grandfather. The chant of the lullaby was the same for all of them. *I am here, I love you. There's nothing to be afraid of.* Miranda's mother was Miranda grown-up, and she wasn't always a pillar of strength.

Miranda could hear the serene strains of classical music coming from Grandma's room—Miranda's room. Her grandmother was being sheltered, comforted, in her grandaughter's room. Under their roof. If her grandfather knew, he would be glad.

"Miranda, my daughter, my friend!" exclaimed her mother. Her violet eyes were luminous and tender. Miranda's heart expanded like an accordion.

TEN

Miranda awoke the next morning to the ring of the telephone. Body heavy with sleep, mind still roving in dreams, she heard her father shuffle past her room to answer. Her eyes wandered to the apple-green dresser, the lopsided rocking chair, the bookshelves, Raggedy Ann, the Monopoly. She wiggled her toes against the sheets and allowed the day to slip in upon her. Sunday was the best time to think. Miranda called it talking to the bed —it was better than bedtime, for sleep did not break your thoughts.

She thought about yesterday. Greta Garbo, Grandma's pride in her new job, the airing of her mother's grief. Miranda sat up and propped herself against the pillow. Though the shades were drawn, a buttery yellow light filtered through. She ran her fingers through her hair. Her hand came out quick as a lick. Miranda felt different. It wasn't only the hair. Somehow other things seemed different, too. Grandma's living here had made a change in the way Miranda viewed things. In the way she viewed herself. And her mother. They shared things in common, yet each needed to be her own person. Each had her private dreams.

Again Miranda looked around her room, at the friendly furniture, the dog-eared books, the familiar crack on the ceiling, the dopey lovable Raggedy Ann. Today, on this Sunday, Miranda loved her room. It was a nest, a cradle, a diary of her past.

Suddenly Miranda wasn't longing for abrupt changes. Growing up at times was like being on a sled that goes careening down an icy slope while you hold on, praying for an embankment of soft snow to slacken the dizzy speed. And at other times it dragged with crocodile feet. Take one giant step forward . . . and two tiny steps back. Growing up was like that. It didn't happen in one straight line. You lunged forward and then inched back.

"Mir-ran-da."

Miranda listened to her mother beckoning from the kitchen. The yodeling summons sounded like a Christmas carol.

"Coming," she called back.

Dad was at the table eating apple pancakes and talking to her mother. "It was a man who called from Warren's Garden Center. He said that Grandma had ordered a dogwood tree—for Grandpa's grave—and to tell her that it had been planted."

Dogwood was Grandpa's favorite tree, thought Miranda. *It will be like the little white goat he had as a pet when he was a boy, like the little white goat in the lullaby he used to sing. The dogwood will grow and keep him company.* She looked at her mother. Their eyes met.

"Where is Grandma?" Miranda asked. "Isn't she having breakfast?"

"She's already had some. She was up real early. I guess she's in her room straightening up."

Miranda turned to find her, and in the hallway they bumped into each other. Grandma, dressed in coat and scarf, was carrying her suitcase. She stood at the doorway of the kitchen.

"Well, everybody, I'm ready to leave."

"What do you mean?" Miranda asked.

"I'm going home," Grandma announced.

"You can't do that," said Miranda. "This *is* your home."

Miranda's mother came over, lifted the suitcase from her mother's hand and set it on the floor. She took her mother's elbow. "Miranda's right," she said, and then added, "Mama, aren't you happy here?"

"It isn't that, Hannah. No, it isn't that. But the time has come for me to go back to my own house. Every living thing wants its bit of space. And needs it. Here, I'm a transplant. My roots, my traces, my memories, are there."

"I understand," Miranda's father said, "but it gives us such peace of mind to have you under our roof."

Grandma smiled. "I guess I can take care of myself. Mr. Castleway called me a spunky old lady. Funny, I don't feel old, but I guess that's how it is. Old age startles you. One day someone calls you old, and you know that's what you are. But, young or old, I can still lead my own life. And since I'm working now, money will be no problem. My time will be usefully filled."

Miranda wanted to cry out, "Grandma, don't leave us. Don't leave me." But she knew it would not be for Grandma's sake, but for her own. She understood her grandmother's need for a place of her own, for her own independence. Space in which to act rather than a confined space in which to be acted upon.

Grandma picked up her suitcase. "Miranda, will you walk me home?"

Miranda looked at her parents. They gave no sign of further protest. Their eyes were understanding and encouraging.

Her grandparents' house was only a few blocks away. She and Grandma walked along Riverside Drive. The oak trees in the park had turned yellow, the maples red. Batches of leaves lay helter-skelter on the ground like patches of burnished leather. The warm air had that dry autumn smell, like a sachet tucked in a drawer of linen. It was Indian summer.

"Looks like winter will never come," said Miranda.

Her grandmother smiled. "But it will."

In front of her building, Grandma paused at the door. Miranda stood still, but her hands clutched her side.

"We haven't been here . . . since Grandpa died," she said.

"That isn't quite true, Miranda. I have."

"When?"

"When I went out for walks, I often came here. It was peaceful to be in my own place and think of Grandpa and sort my memories and thoughts."

What did she do when she came here? Did she look at the bed where Grandpa died? Or sort the old photographs in the top drawer of his bureau?

As her grandmother spoke, Miranda realized

that you never tell anybody everything. Though she and her grandmother confided in each other, trusted each other, there are things you tell only one person—yourself.

They went into the lobby. The name plate on the letter box said "Leonard Goldsmith."

"Grandpa's name is still on," Miranda whispered.

Grandma fished out her key. The box was filled with mail. Eagerly she shuffled through the letters as they waited for the elevator. She tapped her foot, impatient to be home. Upstairs, as her grandmother inserted the key into the lock, Miranda's heart was beating wildly. It was hard for her to face the apartment without Grandpa. As the door opened, the familiar smell of vanilla, ironing, and geraniums lingered, but the smell of Grandpa's pipe was gone.

Grandma walked through the living room and carefully laid her suitcase on the bed in the bedroom. She pulled up the drawn shades and opened the windows. Then she went back to the kitchen, took the watering can from its shelf and began watering the geraniums. The dry soil sucked the water greedily. Miranda watched her. There was a deliberateness, a rightness, a serenity in all of her movements. She belonged here; she fit; she was inhabiting her own skin.

On the kitchen counter, in the empty fruit bowl, lay Grandpa's pipe. Miranda picked it up and turned it round in her hand. How long, she wondered, would his fingerprints remain?

"Miranda, can I make you a cup of tea?"

Miranda had a strong hunch that Grandma wanted to be alone.

"No, thanks, Grandma. I have to run. Jenny is picking me up at twelve. We're going to the first show of *Bride of Frankenstein*. We never did get to see it yesterday. I'll take a rain check, though, on that tea. Tomorrow, after school?"

Grandma smiled. "It's a date. Make it after four. When I finish work." She pronounced the word *work* as if she'd just invented it.

As Miranda went into the elevator and waved good-bye, she felt a pang of sadness. It felt odd leaving Grandma all alone in that apartment. She would have lonely moments. But Grandma, planted in the doorway, looked so sturdy, so animated, so spunky, that by the time the elevator reached the ground floor, that pang was gone. Grandma had the strength to lead a life of her own, and when she needed them, they would be there.

Miranda ran home, for no reason, except that a prodding inside her made her want to run. October whispered in the autumn leaves. The wind breathed on her neck. Today was Sunday, almost noon, the thirty-first of October. Tomorrow was November first. There were so many things to do.

Miranda had forgotten her key and had to ring. Her mother answered.

"Do you have a minute, Miranda?" she asked at the door.

Oh, no, thought Miranda. *Some chore coming up, like "Would you mind going down again to pick up the* Sunday Times?"

"What is it, Mom?"

"Come with me. It won't take long, I promise."

Miranda followed her into Grandma's room. The room looked exactly as it had when Sonya occupied it. Except, on the bed, lay Grandma's patchwork quilt. *She must have forgotten it in her hurry*, thought Miranda.

"Grandma left a note for you," said her mother, pointing to a small white envelope on top of the quilt.

Miranda opened it. The note read: "Miranda, this quilt is for you. In your new room. Thank you for helping me to do what I wanted. Love, Grandma."

Miranda glanced at her mother, who stood in the doorway, as if to allow Miranda her own space. To grow up. Miranda's eyes swept around her new room. It was large and filled with light. Her eyes swung down to the patchwork quilt with its swatches of outgrown dresses.

Each familiar piece was like a portion of her life, an experience. The shapes fit and belonged together: they formed the pattern. From a distance the quilt looked seamless, without joinings. But up close, Miranda could see and touch the intricate little stitches Grandma had made.

The ripe sun flooded the room. The diamond-shaped pieces of the quilt, reds, blues, yellows, and orange were melting into each other. Miranda raised her hand through her hair. The black patch on her nail was almost grown out. It was almost time to be waiting for snow.

The Author

Toby Talbot, a native New Yorker, has been a professor of Spanish and the education editor for *El Diario*. She has also written and directed a film, translated several books from the Spanish, edited *The World of the Child* (a collection of readings on childhood), and written numerous books for children. The Talbots and their three daughters travel extensively.